LIFE ON A DIFFERENT PLANET
A CLIMATE CRISIS HANDBOOK

by Randi Hacker

Illustrations by Ron Barrett

Home Planet Books

Burlington, Vermont
www.onionriverpress.com

FOR US ALL.

LIFE ON A DIFFERENT PLANET

Copyright 2020, by Randi Hacker.
All rights reserved including theme parks and those of translation into a foreign language. No part of this publication may be reproduced or transmitted in any form or by any means, without permission in writing from the author except, of course, by a reviewer who may quote brief passages in a review to be printed or loaded either up or down.

For information, email publisher@homeplanetbooks.com
www.homeplanetbooks.com

Home Planet Books is a publishing company located on Earth.

Designed by Carolyn Brown and Jon Bransky

Illustrations © 2020 by Ron Barrett

Life on a Different Planet/Randi Hacker

       ISBN: 978-0-578-62406-8 paperback

       ISBN: 978-1-949066-56-2 eBook

     1. Climate Change — Children
     2. Earth — Non-fiction
     3. Earthlings — All

First Edition: 2020

This book is printed on paper that is responsibly sourced from sustainably-managed forests.

AUTHOR'S NOTE

President Obama recently tweeted these words:

Barack Obama
@BarackObama

"We've seen all too terribly the consequences of those who denied warnings of a pandemic. We can't afford any more consequences of climate denial. All of us, especially young people, have to demand better of our government at every level and vote this fall."

HE'S RIGHT.

And reports about the improvement in air quality and water quality abound in the news these days. In fact, when we all stayed home during the pandemic, carbon emissions dropped 17%.

So, if the coronavirus epidemic has taught us anything, it has taught us two things:

– **Preemptive action makes the difference.**
– **Our Earth is so willing to heal if we give her a chance.**

LET'S REMEMBER THIS AS WE MOVE FORWARD.

FOREWORD

Dear Fellow Earthlings,

My name is Siri Dunn, I am 13 years old and I am scared for the future of our planet. I live on the side of a mountain in Morrisville, Vermont. My family grows most of our food, including chicken and vegetables. I am writing an article for my local newspaper addressing climate change.

The earth is rapidly changing. Temperatures are going up and ecosystems are collapsing. Many young people don't know. That's why I'm so grateful for this book. Youth need to know about climate change and what the impact will be, so it makes me very glad to know that someone is addressing that. It's important that we realize what we've started and how it will affect all life on earth. That's exactly what this book does. Adults have known about climate change since 1988 and they chose to do very little. They left it up to our generation. This book encourages us to act, and it's important that we do. So I'm acting. I'm acting because I want a safe, clean future for myself and my children and my children's children. This book inspired me. We can all do something. We can make an effort to drive less, and use less plastic. We can compost our food waste, and make our voices heard. There is always a way for you to act. This is my way.

This is the planet you will be inheriting someday. In a way, it's already yours, and your planet needs your help. It's time to get going.

#uturnbeginswithyou
Love,

Siri

Welcome to the END of the WORLD.

WHEN YOU THINK ABOUT IT, when you really sit down and think about it, you can see that the end of this world might not be an altogether bad thing.

In this world, we humans have been destructive in the extreme:

- **We cut down rain forests.**
- **Our oil spills destroy fragile ecosystems.**
- **Our fossil-fuel burning engines pollute our air.**
- **The toxic waste we dump pollutes our water.**
- **Our factory farms are cruel and add methane to the atmosphere.**
- **Our CO2 emissions are threatening the survival of all life on Earth including us.**

But it doesn't have to continue that way. Earth is your planet too. You can be in the vanguard of a force that creates a new world, a world in which you do better than we've done before.

**ITS A BIG JOB.
TIME TO GET STARTED.**

LIFE ON A DIFFERENT PLANET

EARTH 2037

You wake up sweating. You're only allowed to have your air conditioning on five hours a day and your five hours ended about five hours ago. They're getting closer to perfecting those total solar and zero HFC units they keep promising but until then, you will sweat.

You raise your blackout shade. The thermometer outside your window registers 106 degrees. Your bedside clock says it's 7:30 PM. Time to start your night.

You get out of bed and throw on the coolest clothes you have, fasten on your headlamp and walk outside. It's not quite dark – the sun has slipped below the horizon and the western sky is orange and blue and pink, and white with heat. You wave to Ms. Lyons who is just getting home. She works the day shift at the hospital.

Your mother and father and grandmother and grandfather are out there already checking on the garden after yesterday's storm. The damage is not too bad, they tell you. A few tomatoes knocked off the vine, some

potato plants flattened, weren't we lucky that last night's hurricane was only a Category 2 and not one of those Category 5 storms you hear about. And there was only 6 inches of rain instead of 40, adds your father.

Your grandmother sits up on her knees, looks at you and begins to cry.

"I'm sorry," she says. "On behalf of my whole generation, I'm sorry that we didn't act soon enough. We failed you."

Your grandfather pats her on the back.

This is not the first time she's apologized. For a second, you let the anger flare up because yeah, that generation did fail you and you do blame her and not just her, of course, but everyone who didn't do enough back in the 20th century when there was still a chance to cap the heat at a 1.5 degree rise but she looks so sad and you know that she has to work just as hard now as you do in addition to feeling guilty so you smile at her and say, "Well, at least you joined 100 Grannies."

She sniffles and nods.

You open the doors to the chicken coop which is really your grandfather's old Hummer. The chickens hop out. You throw them some grain then collect eggs from the nests all over the back and passenger seats but not the driver's seat. They're not allowed to nest

there. Grandpa sometimes still sits in it with his elbow resting on the open window and his right hand draped over the steering wheel, an unlit cigarette between the first two fingers. He's had that cigarette since 2020.

After a breakfast of eggs from your chickens and a slice of tomato, you set off for school.

It's weird walking up 6th Street when, up until last week, you always walked along 5th. But now 5th is under the ocean, so yeah.

An electric car slides up beside you. The window rolls down.

"Want a ride?" asks your friend, Ruchira who came to your town from South Asia in the First Mass Migration.

"Sure," you say.

You hop in. Ruchira's mother cruises down the road listening to the radio.

"This morning at the Global Cooperation Summit, the President of the United States joined other world leaders in an agreement to manage the mass migrations. 'We must all open our borders and welcome those of us most affected by the crisis,' she said."

You slide past the ruined buildings of the factory farm. Now it's 10 small farms. Farmer Mark waves to you from the gate. You wave back. Ruchira's family is vegan but your family gets its meat and milk from him.

You glide past downtown. Predictions are that the water level will not rise enough to flood the Tenth Street Promenade but no one knows, really. Right now, a few of the windows are lit up and the line at Starbucks stretches all the way to the Third Fifth Public Bank.

Three deer at the edge of the second growth forest look up as your car rolls silently past then go back to their grazing.

Just before the abandoned airfield with the empty hulks of airplanes looming darkly on the runway, the car turns and joins the drop-off line at Greta Thunberg Middle School.

You and Ruchira get out of the car.

"Make good choices," calls Ruchira's mother steering the car away. You and Ruchira head into the building. The school thermometer says it's 98 degrees, only eight degrees cooler though the sunset an hour ago.

Your classes today are World Climate History, Solar Science, Math, Lunch, English and Nature Art. After school, you play your clarinet in the band at the big basketball game against Bill McKibben Middle School. Your team wins by 10 points.

When you leave the school, the temperature has dropped to 70 degrees and there's a gentle breeze that feels great on your skin. The streets are alive with people who have come out to enjoy the cool air. Your grandmother told you that, when she was a kid, 70 was sometimes the high during the day.

By the time you walk home, have your dinner and do your homework, the eastern sky has begun to lighten.

You wish your parents a good day and go to bed.

You put on your pajamas and lower your blackout shade just as a sun the color of lava boils up over the horizon. The temperature has already climbed to 95 degrees.

You turn on the air exchanger and lie down. You stick to your sheets but what else is new?

You close your eyes.

LET'S FACE IT: THINGS HERE ON EARTH COULD BE BETTER

You probably already know this.

Things are changing on our home planet because there's too much carbon dioxide, CO**2**, and methane[1] trapped in our atmosphere.

CO**2** is a natural byproduct of carbon-based lifeforms. Trees and green plants remove it from the atmosphere and use it to photosynthesize.

That's the carbon cycle and it's a beautiful system. But, at the moment, it's terribly out of balance.

We humans are clever carbon-based lifeforms and we have invented cool technologies that make it possible for us to produce way more CO**2** and methane[2] than any other carbon-based lifeform has ever produced in the history of carbon-based lifeforms.

Those trapped gases are heating this planet up.

---

1 Yes, that's in a fart. But it's also a gas that is released whenever humans drill for natural gas.
2 Ronald Reagan, the 40th President of the United States, tried to blame excess methane on cow farts, but then again, he blamed smog on trees and called ketchup a vegetable.

Ten years ago, scientists told us that a 1.5-degree Celsius rise in Earth's average temperature would have a devastating effect on life on Earth. Ten years ago, we might have been able to cap it at that.

But we didn't act and now we are being told that the Earth's average temperature could increase by 5 degrees. But no one really knows.

Five degrees might not sound like a lot but, historically, it has taken our planet roughly 5,000 years to see a 5 degree rise in temperature.

We have accomplished that more than 20x faster. This is not something to be proud of.

This rise in temperature is changing Earth into a different planet, one that is not as hospitable to humans and other Earthlings. The hotter it gets, the harder it will be to raise food. The hotter it gets, the wilder the weather. The hotter it gets, the less water. The hotter it gets, the warmer the oceans. And the hotter it gets, the higher the oceans rise.

Not every Earthling will survive.

BUT HERE'S THE THING:

if we act now, there's a chance that we can prevent the planet from getting even hotter. And if we prevent the planet from getting even hotter, there's a chance that our only home planet will recover. Just take a look at how quickly the air and water cleaned themselves when we stopped driving so much and stopped flying so much during the pandemic. It shows how willing Earth is to heal if we just give her the chance.

SURVIVAL BOILS DOWN TO BEATING THE ODDS

People say that the odds are stacked against us. That doesn't matter. Throughout Earth's long history, the odds have been beaten time again. In fact, Earth beats the odds just by being here.

Odds of finding a habitable planet

7,000,000,000,000,000,000 to 1.

THAT'S 7 QUINTILLION.
And yet, here we are.

ARE YOU AN ANTHRO SUPREMACIST?

Anthro is the Greek word for 'man', which here means 'human' and a supremacist is someone who believes themselves superior to everyone else and, therefore, deserves to have everything the way they want it to be.

Anthro supremacists have a long history of thinking the Earth is theirs and theirs alone. They are not good sharers. They use up more resources, claim the territories of other Earthlings as their own and kill more other Earthlings for sport and profit than any other Earthlings.

Anthro supremacism plays the major part in what is throwing our system off balance.

IT'S NOT A FIGHT

Once there was a Roman emperor named Caligula who marched his army from Italy to France and straight into the ocean to fight Neptune the God of the Sea by slashing their swords through the waves. Caligula declared himself the victor but he didn't win; he and his army just got wet.

You can't fight the ocean.

You can't fight climate change.

You CAN stand up for the planet.

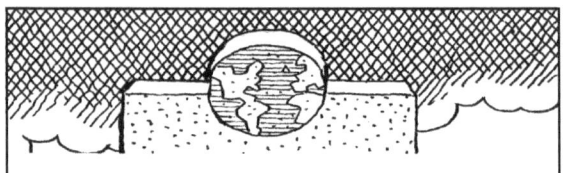

WEATHER VS. CLIMATE

Don't confuse weather with climate.

THE WEATHER is what happens over a short time: a day, a week.

THE CLIMATE is the weather of a place averaged over time.

HOW ON EARTH DO YOU MEASURE EARTH'S AVERAGE TEMPERATURE?

Temperatures have been rising steadily since the Industrial Revolution which began more than 200 years ago. That's when humans began burning CO_2 in unprecedented amounts. In 1880, humans began keeping records of the Earth's average temperature. We've been keeping records ever since. The average global temperature has risen .085 degrees Celsius (1.4 degrees Fahrenheit) in just 139 years.

> **❝ Habitats and species on the brink of extinction can recover if given a chance ❞**
> – JANE GOODALL

do the math

If it takes Earth 5,000 years to get hotter by 5 degrees, how long would it take Earth to raise the heat .085 degrees if we humans did not interfere?

Show your work.

#UTURNBEGINSWITHYOU

YOU'RE ANGRY.
You have every right to be.

Previous generations have failed you and continue to fail you by not acting at once to ensure a viable future for our only home planet.

Why didn't they act when there was more time? Didn't they care?

A lot of them did—and do – care about Earth. And your future.

But a lot of them did – and do – care more about money. They care more about economics than they do about ecosystems.

There's a flaw in this reasoning, of course: If you haven't got a healthy planet, where on Earth are you going to spend that money?

So yeah.

You should be good and angry.

Go ahead and stomp.

And scream into a pillow.

And grind your teeth.

And get together with your friends and vent.

And tell your parents and grandparents how you feel.

And then get over it. There's no time for anger. There's work to do and it's up to you. You are inheriting a badly damaged planet.

GET ANGRY.
GET OVER IT.
GET TO WORK.

If you think it's not fair that it's up to you, you're right. But, as Scar famously points out in Disney's Lion King:

"Life's not fair, is it?"

> **❝** Our house is on fire and we know what to do to put it out. **❞**
> – GRETA THUNBERG

Zero C For Me, See?
(ZeroC. Like ZeroG. Only with Carbon.)

Government and industry and corporations say they can't possibly cut carbon emissions to zero, not even by 2030. They just can't do it.

BUT YOU CAN.

You can start cutting your own carbon emissions down to ZeroC* anytime you want.

YOU COULD START NOW.

You could invite your family.
Your family could invite another family.
And so on.

Because #uturnbeginswithyou.

*Well not zero. Don't be silly. Carbon-based lifeforms add CO_2 to the atmosphere every time they breathe out. Humans alone add 3 billion tons a year. But the carbon we breathe out is the same CO_2 we ingest in the vegetables we eat, the very CO_2 the plants use in photosynthesis. That's called carbon neutrality and it's ZeroC at its very best.

ADAPTATION = SURVIVAL

When a lifeform adapts, it makes itself able to live in an environment. Species that don't adapt, don't survive.

Lifeforms can do this two ways: biologically or behaviorally. Biological adaptation involves body parts.

A Bactrian camel can store fat in its humps that it can turn into water and energy to use on long, hot, dry treks across the desert.

Behavioral adaptation is more of a Do-It-Yourself thing. It involves action and decision-making skill. Humans are particularly good at this.

Humans may be mammals but we aren't really suited to living in the cold. We have no fur. So we adapted by making clothes out of other animals' fur.

It's time for another DIY behavioral adaptation, one that allows us to survive in an environment that is not going to be as hospitable to us or to many other Earthlings or to the ecosystems we rely on.

ADAPTATION TIPS TO GET YOU STARTED

- **Go out in the cooler parts of the day: morning, evening and night.**
- **Sit still.**
- **Use a fan.**
- **Wear a hat.**
- **Lie flat on the grass on your back with your arms and your legs spread wide.**
- **Walk.**
- **Sweat.**

Apply the Physician's Oath "First, do no harm" to every action.

And here's the important part: we must adapt in ways that release no more ancient carbon into our atmosphere.

And this will be hard.
But it's the hard that will make it great.

ASK YOURSELF: WHAT CAN I DO TODAY THAT IS LESS HARMFUL?

Can I live without air conditioning?

You'll have to sweat more. That's the bottom line. Air conditioners in the USA add about 100 million tons of CO_2 to the atmosphere each year.

Can I walk to a friend's house instead of being driven?
Cars and trucks account for 24 pounds of CO_2 per gallon of gas.

And, if I can't walk to a friend's house, can I play at home for Earth's sake?
Playing at home means no driving. That's Zero C for me see? in real time.

Can I give up flying?
Flights produced nearly 915 million tons of CO_2 worldwide in 2018. The USA is responsible for almost half of the entire world's aircraft CO_2 emissions.

Can I stop mowing my lawn with a gas-powered mower and stop blowing my leaves and snow with gas-powered devices?

A gas-powered mower produces as much CO2 as 40 cars do in an hour.
And electric mowers are better but you still have to plug them in. Even though in 2019 the US got more power from renewable sources than ever before, much of our electricity still comes from sources that burn fossil fuels, sources such as coal-powered power plants.

Can I dry my laundry on a clothes line or drying rack?
Washing your clothes and putting them in the dryer adds 5.28 pounds of CO2 to the atmosphere. Washing your clothes and hanging them on a line reduces that to 1.3 pounds.

Can I spend less time on my computer and phone?
Sure, the lithium-ion batteries that power your computer, your cell phone, your electric car, can be recharged and recycled but they're made from resources that have to be mined.

Mining equipment burns fossil fuels. And then the elements that have been mined have to be shipped around the world. The batteries have to be assembled. And the people who assemble them have to drive to work.

The three elements in lithium-ion batteries are cobalt, lithium and graphite. Cobalt mining releases heavy metals like uranium and lead into the groundwater. Mining lithium uses a lot of water – sometimes as much as 2 million gallons per day. And graphite dust pollutes air and soil and water.

In fact, there's one river in one of China's graphite mining districts that is so polluted with graphite, it doesn't even freeze anymore.

Climate change is going to bring drought. In times of drought is this the best way to use our water?

NOW ASK YOURSELF:

Can I do these things every day?

Because it can't be a one-time thing. You can't turn off the air conditioner or sweep the leaves for one afternoon and call it good. You have to do it every day for Earth's sake.

Turning things around requires a commitment from you to adapt the way you think and live so you can survive in a different environment. That's the very definition of behavioral adaptation.

WASH YOUR CLOTHES BY HAND

Here's how:

1. CHECK LABELS. Make sure your clothes can be washed by hand. Even some clothes that say "Dry Clean Only" can be washed by hand but check with your folks first. Don't wash leather or silk.

2. GET YOUR SUPPLIES IN ORDER. You need eco-friendly laundry soap, water and a tub of some sort. You can use a bucket or a basin or the bathtub or the sink. Whatever you use, make sure its clean before you wash your clothes in it.

3. FILL THE TUB WITH WATER. Warm or cold. Not too hot. Add eco-friendly soap and swish around to mix and make bubbles.

4. SORT BY COLOR. You don't want your white things turning red or blue.

5. SORT BY DIRTINESS. Wash dirtier stuff with dirtier stuff. You don't want to add dirt to clothes that are a bit cleaner.

6. DUNK THOSE CLOTHES AND SCRUB AWAY. Use the material of the clothing to scrub itself.

7. KEEP AN EYE ON THE WATER. When it gets murky, pour it out on the driveway or even in the yard. You're using soap that isn't toxic, so it's okay. But don't water the plants with it: even eco-friendly soap will kill them.

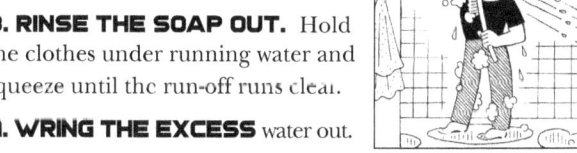

8. RINSE THE SOAP OUT. Hold the clothes under running water and squeeze until the run-off runs clear.

9. WRING THE EXCESS water out.

10. HANG THOSE CLEAN clothes on a line in the sun.

OR YOU COULD JUST WEAR YOUR CLOTHES IN THE SHOWER. Check with the folks first.

You have to LIVE as if LIFE depended on it.
WHICH IT DOES.

#UTURNBEGINSWITHYOU

The choice is simple:
EITHER YOU CONTRIBUTE TO EARTH'S OBITUARY

OR

YOU GIVE OUR HOME PLANET THE CHANCE IT DESERVES TO RECOVER.

IT'S A NO-BRAINER!
Except it really does require a brain.
Happily, you have one.

These days, climate change is the object in a state of motion. You are the external force that acts on it.

GRETA THUNBERG REFUSES TO FLY.

So, when she was invited to speak at a climate conference in New York City, she sailed across the ocean in a solar-powered boat. It took two weeks. A flight would have taken about 8 ½ hours.

USE A RAKE. A leaf-blower engine emits more carbon than a 3-ton automobile. Ditto, chain saws.

CLIMATE CHANGE THROUGH THE YEARS

Earth has a long history of trying on different climates – at times, it has been hot enough for a hippopotamus to live comfortably in England; at times, it has been cold enough for ice to cover 30% of the planet – California was once embedded in ice. But this type of climate change usually occurs in Earth time, that is, slowly, over thousands of years. This is the first time humans have sped it up by contributing to it.

And this is the first time that humans can do something to change it.

Earth. It's your planet now. You can do better than we've done.

COMING SOON TO A PLANET NEAR YOU!

1. ~~STONE AGE~~
2. ~~BRONZE AGE~~
3. ~~IRON AGE~~
4. FOSSIL FUEL AGE ⬅ **WE ARE HERE!**
5. **THE POST-CARBON AGE**

do the math

A flight from London to New York generates about 986 kg of CO_2 per passenger. A trans-Atlantic plane can carry as many as 450 people. How many kgs of CO_2 total does a flight of this size add to our atmosphere? How many pounds?

Now multiply that number by 102,465 which is the approximate number of commercial flights that typically have gone out every day.

Now multiply that number by 365 which is the number of days in a year.

• • • • • • • • • • • •
• 1 kg = 2.2 pounds •
• • • • • • • • • • • •

WORDS OF HONOR

TO MAKE A DIFFERENCE, TO MAKE A REAL DIFFERENCE, YOU HAVE TO TRAIN YOUR BRAIN TO THINK
IN A WHOLE NEW WAY.

Let's call it PC: **Planetarily Correct.**

Start your training by asking yourself how much your every action contributes to raising the temperature of our home planet.

Because, in fact, pretty much every action you take as an early 21st Century human being adds carbon to Earth's atmosphere.

FOR EXAMPLE:

YOU BUY A NEW TOY OR A SHIRT WITH YOUR FAVORITE ANIME CHARACTER ON IT.

- When you eat food or buy clothing or toys that had to be flown in from thousands of miles away, the fossil fuel that was burned to get it here added CO2 to the atmosphere.
- So did the drilling and transport of the fossil fuel itself.
- So did the manufacturing of the toy and clothing and the cultivating of the food.
- So did the fuel burned by the employees getting to their places of work.

YOU CHARGE YOUR PHONE BATTERY.

- Fossil fuel-burning power plants spew enormous amounts of CO2 into the atmosphere.
- Add to that the fossil fuel that is burned bringing the fossil fuel to the plants to be burnt and the CO2 that is released in the mining and drilling of this ancient carbon.*
- And, oh yeah, don't forget the fossil fuel burning vehicles used to bring the employees to their places of employment.

YOU TURN ON THE AIR CONDITIONING BECAUSE IT IS VERY HOT OUTSIDE.

- Air conditioners are major contributors to global warming.
- And then, as always, there's the fossil fuel burned to transport those air conditioners to the store and then to your house.
- Then there's the fossil fuel that was burned to manufacture the materials the air conditioner is composed of and, again, there's the gas burned by the cars the employees drive to their places of work.

YOU EAT A HAMBURGER FOR SCHOOL LUNCH.

- Schools buy meat from factory farms because it's less expensive.
- Factory farms contribute enormous amounts of CO2 to the atmosphere from animal farts to animal manure to the fertilizer and farm equipment needed to grow high energy grain to feed the thousands of pigs, cows and chickens to transporting the meat all over the country.

* To say nothing of the methane, another greenhouse gas that absorbs even more heat than CO2.

PC THINKING IS ALL ABOUT LAYERS.

Ask yourself these PC Questions before you do or buy anything.
- Where does it come from?
- How did it get here?
- How was it made?
- Do you need it or do you just want it?

Look at your every action. How close to ZeroC are you? Can you get any closer?
- Start with one thing. Buy local food.
- Add another. Walk to a friend's house.
- And another. Stay away from the water park.
- And another. Use a clothes line…and so on…

AND FOR EACH ONE YOU DO, GIVE YOURSELF YOUR WORD OF HONOR THAT YOU WILL CONTINUE DOING IT.

Because it can't just be one time; it has to be from now on.

Doing this from now on means that you are not only giving our only home planet the chance it deserves to recover, you are also guaranteeing that future generations won't point a finger at you* and say,

"Why didn't you act? Didn't you care?"

* For this at any rate

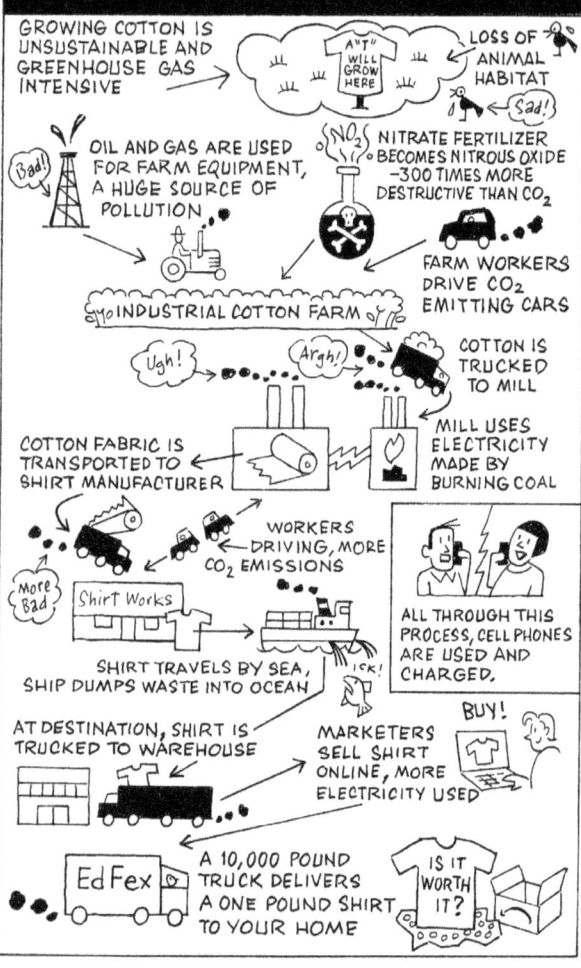

HERE ARE SOME WORDS OF HONOR TO JUMPSTART YOUR PC THINKING.

 I GIVE MY WORD OF HONOR that I will not be an Anthro Supremacist. Humans are not the only Earthlings that call this planet home.

 I GIVE MY WORD OF HONOR that I will be PC. I will think of the planet in every any action I take.

 I GIVE MY WORD OF HONOR that I will live small and stay home. What does this mean? It means less driving. It means less flying. It means being alone a bit more. It means amusing yourself. You did this during the pandemic for the sake of your own health; now do it for the sake of your planet's health.

 I GIVE MY WORD OF HONOR to welcome all kinds of Earthlings from places that become inhospitable to them. Not every Earthling will survive on our different planet. As the climate gets hotter and the glaciers melt and the oceans rise, there will be places on Earth where habitation is no longer possible for humans and other Earthlings. This will cause mass migrations. Our actions today can affect the rise in temperature but not right away. We must open our arms and yards to Earthlings whose homes disappear.

I GIVE MY WORD OF HONOR that I will appreciate how lucky I am to live on Earth. Humans have been looking for extraterrestrial life throughout their history. But, so far, we have found not one single other planet that supports life.

 **I GIVE MY WORD OF HONOR** to take a little time every day to appreciate the wonder of this. And while you're at it, take a little time to think about this again: The odds were stacked against the rise of life on Earth and yet…here we all are.

 **I GIVE MY WORD OF HONOR** that I will make myself heard. Let the adults know that you need their help. There are several ways to do this:
- Write a Letter to the Editor of your local paper. *(More about this on the next page.)*
- Stage a school climate strike.
- Talk to your parents.
- Make presentations at eco-events.
- Tell your friends about **#uturnbeginswithyou**.

HOW TO WRITE A LETTER TO THE EDITOR
(LTE)
A letter to the editor is a statement of your opinion about something that's going on. Anyone can write a letter to the editor about anything. This is known as free speech, a First Amendment right for all Americans.

In your letter, you can say what you think about the way people in power are ignoring the reality of climate change so they can make money and how this makes you feel about your future. If you're scared, say so. If you're angry, say so. If you're doing something to bring your carbon footprint closer to ZeroC say so. Be polite and firm.

Sending a letter to the editor does not, however, mean that your letter will definitely be published. Editors receive loads of letters every day and they can't print them all.

But that doesn't mean you shouldn't write them and send them, partly because writing can help you feel better, partly because the more letters you write and send, the more likely you are to see one of them in print but mostly because the more letters you get in print, the more people will read what you have to say which is what you want because...

...ultimately, the function of a Letter to the Editor is make your voice heard.

IMPORTANT NOTE: If you are under 18, please show your letter to your parents first. You want them to know what you're saying plus your local paper might require their permission.

SAMPLE LTE

To the Editor:

A lot of us kids are doing all we can to reduce our carbon footprints; we are playing with our next-door-neighbors instead of driving to a friend's, we are not flying in planes, we are hanging our clothes on a line. All these things are good but we're still kids and we need more adults to do things. We need more adults to stop drilling. We need more adults to stop fracking. We need more adults to close down factory farms. We need more adults to invest in renewable energy. And we need more adults to stand beside us as we move into an uncertain future.

Sincerely yours,
Your Name, Your Age
Your City and State

I GIVE MY WORD OF HONOR that I will get to know my farmer. If you don't want what you eat to come with a lot of carbon baggage, buy it from someone closer to home. Shop at a farmers market. Be your own farmer.

And if you choose to eat meat, choose meat that lived a freer life.

FACTORY FARMS

Earthlings have always hunted and eaten other Earthlings. That's just a fact of life. At some point, we humans began domesticating other Earthlings. Instead of hunting them and eating them, we raised them – we took care of them; we protected them from other predators and then we ate them ourselves. Up until the 1960s, farms were small and usually run by a family, maybe for generations.

But the human population grew very fast and small farms could not keep up with demand.

So scientists and agriculturalists invented the factory farm where thousands of pigs, cows, chickens and goats can be confined in small spaces and given high fat foods, drugs and hormones to make them grow bigger, faster.

In addition to being no way to treat a fellow Earthling, factory farms add massive quantities of global warming gases to the atmosphere.

HERE'S HOW:

- Thousands of carbon-based lifeforms produce thousands of farts – which includes those of the farmhands. Each fart contains methane, a greenhouse gas that has 20 times the global warming power as CO2.
- Farms that raise thousands of carbon-based lifeforms require enormous amounts of fossil fuel energy to operate.

In all, factory farms are responsible for:

9% of all human-generated carbon emissions
37% of all methane emissions
65% of all nitrous oxide emissions

IF YOU KNOW YOUR FARMER, you know how your meat was raised.
IF YOU KNOW YOUR BUTCHER, you know how your meat was slaughtered.

I GIVE MY WORD OF HONOR to want less. Not having everything is the new having everything. The less you buy, the less fossil fuel it takes to get it to you. Ask yourself: what can you live without?

 I GIVE MY WORD OF HONOR to sweat more. Turn off that air conditioner. Make a fan. Lie still in the shade. Drink water.

 **I GIVE MY WORD OF HONOR** to be a little dirtier. Droughts are coming. Make adjustments to your water usage now. You don't have to bathe every day. You don't have to wash your clothes as often. You don't have to flush the toilet after every pee. You don't have to leave the water running while you brush your teeth or do the dishes. You especially don't have to water the lawn.

ONE US GALLON = 3.785411784 LITERS
1 LITER = .26 GALLONS

- A typical American uses 80-100 gallons of water a day.
- A typical Japanese uses 250 liters a day.
- A typical Botswanan uses 50-100 liters per day
- Can you live one day on only 50-100 liters of water?

---

do the math

A typical American shower uses 2.5 gallons per minute.

A low-flow shower uses 2.0 gallons per minute.

How long is your shower? Multiply the number of minutes by 2.5 or 2.0. How much water does your shower send down the drain?

Start Your Own Climate Victory Garden

During WWII, due to food shortages and to help the war effort, people grew what they called Victory Gardens. You can grow a Climate Victory Garden in your yard. Don't have a yard? Grow something in a big pot on your deck or balcony. No balcony? Get a plot in a community garden. When your vegetables and fruit are ripe, pick them and walk them into the kitchen. Pretty close to ZeroC.

Food Not Lawns

Climate change comes with drought. It's part of the package. Watering the grass is not the best use of our water. We don't eat grass.[1]
So...Dig up your lawn.[2]
Plant food.
Water it instead.

Start A School Garden

If there isn't a garden at your school, start one.

1. Talk to your friends and find out who's interested.
2. Find out who's willing to make a commitment to work.
3. Find some adult partners. Science teachers are most likely to say yes to this. As are people from a local food co-op or organic market.
4. Go see the principal to find out what you need to do to turn a piece of the school property into a garden. It will involve some paperwork.
5. Come up with a Garden Plan.
6. Make a work roster.
7. Work.
8. Harvest.
9. Eat.
10. Sell your produce at the local farmers market. Use the money to buy things that will bring your school closer to ZeroC.[3]

---

1 If we were horses...well, this would be a different book.
2 Check with the folks first.
3 Many schools with gardens sell their produce at local farmers markets. You can too. It will involve paperwork.

I GIVE MY WORD OF HONOR to be as ZeroC as a 21st century human possibly can be.

- I will air dry my clothing.
- I will not blow dry my hair.
- I will never use a leaf blower.
- I won't ride on a Jet Ski.
- I won't visit theme parks.
- If I decide to keep my lawn, I will mow it with a reel mower.

ZeroC in the 21ST C.

ARE WE HAVING FUN YET?

A lot of things we humans do to amuse ourselves are carbon beasts. Theme parks add hundreds of thousands of pounds of carbon dioxide to the atmosphere through the energy it takes to run them and the transportation it takes to get humans there. Water parks are the worst. Guess why?

If you said, "Drought. Duh!" you're right. Burning ancient carbon and using water just for amusement is about as non-PC as it gets.

I GIVE MY WORD OF HONOR that I will be patient. Slow is the new fast. The u-turn is not going to happen next week or next month or next year. It might not even happen in the next 20 years. But what you do now will affect the future.

 **I GIVE MY WORD OF HONOR** that I will live as if life depended on it. Which it does.

 **I GIVE MY WORD OF HONOR** to give up plastic. Every plastic bag, every plastic toy, every plastic water bottle, every PVC pipe and walking cast and Lunchable package, in short, every plastic thing, adds carbon to the atmosphere. The manufacture of one pound of PET plastic releases as much as three pounds of CO_2 into the atmosphere. Emissions from plastics could add as much as 56 gigatons of CO_2 to the atmosphere between 2019 and 2050. That's 56 billion tons which is 50 times more than the yearly emissions of all the coal plants in the US. emissions of all the coal plants in the US.

Bottlenose Dolphin

> **Minecraft** is the best-selling video game of all time. And the one with the biggest carbon footprint. Its worldwide CO2 emissions total a whopping 1,322,772,000 pounds.
>
> Because a Minecraft game takes about 120 hours to complete, it also has the highest average CO2 emission per player: 6.6 pounds.
>
> In the US, 112 million people play Minecraft every month. If every player finishes the game, how many pounds of CO2 do they add to the atmosphere per month? Per year?
>
> Show your work.

do the math

WHEN IN DOUBT, OFFSET!
Offset is a way to balance things.
DEVELOP YOUR OWN CARBON-OFFSET SYSTEM

Say the government puts a cap on the amount of CO2 a certain type of business can add to the atmosphere and say one of these businesses always goes over that limit and another always stays under. The first business can buy carbon offsets, or carbon credits, from the second business. You can apply this business model to your own life but the trick is you have to buy your carbon credits from yourself. Evaluate everything you do by its carbon footprint. The things that are closer to ZeroC, go into a credit column; the things that require more fossil fuel, go into a debit column. Then you negotiate with yourself over how much debit your credit can offset.

For example, you really need to use the clothes dryer because it's raining and there's a certain shirt you absolutely must wear when you address the PTA about replacing the annual car wash fundraiser with something less-water and gas-intensive and that shirt is currently wet and you don't have time to hang it outside to dry. Besides, it's raining. Do you have enough credits in your ZeroC column to offset the 5.29109 pounds of CO_2 that a dryer pumps into the air with every load?

Keep a running total. Put it on the fridge. Invite your family to add theirs.

CREDIT	DEBIT
✓ Hung the clothes on line	✓ Used the dryer for Caitlin's party
✓ Turned off the AC off for 12 hours	✓ Drove to the Renaissance Festival
✓ Walked to school	
✓ Did not go to Worlds of Water Fun for vacation	
✓ Talked Dad into selling the leaf blower on e-bay *I was going to do it anyway! –Dad*	
✓ Got rid of the lawn and planted a victory garden.	
✓ Wrote a Letter to the Editor	
✓ Sweated.	

The object, of course, is to always have more in your credit column than you do in your debit column.

THE LESS CO2 YOU SPEW THE COOLER FOR THOSE WHO COME AFTER YOU.

CAREERS

Why not make your work be work that works for the future of our only home planet? Write down and draw some ZeroC career paths you might like to follow.

Draw your ZeroC career path here.

ADD YOUR OWN WORDS OF HONOR.
HONOR YOUR WORD.

I GIVE MY WORD OF HONOR

I GIVE MY WORD OF HONOR

I GIVE MY WORD OF HONOR

I GIVE MY WORD OF HONOR

I GIVE MY WORD OF HONOR

I GIVE MY WORD OF HONOR

I GIVE MY WORD OF HONOR

I GIVE MY WORD OF HONOR

I GIVE MY WORD OF HONOR

I GIVE MY WORD OF HONOR

RESOURCES

LIVING ON A DIFFERENT PLANET

Here are some websites to help you and your family adapt to and thrive here in our new world.

Low Carbon Activities to Do at Home
https://www.gokid.mobi/activities-for-kids-to-reduce-carbon-footprint/

Sierra Club Gardening Tips
These links are about gardening in the pandemic but it pertains just as pertinently to gardening during another crisis: climate change:

https://www.sierraclub.org/sierra/pandemic-gardening-kids-101

https://www.sierraclub.org/sierra/9-ways-get-your-pandemic-victory-garden-ground?suppress=true&utm_source=greenlife&utm_medium=email&utm_campaign=newsletter

Xeriscaping: Drought-hardy Gardening
Some xeriscaping tips:
https://www.gardeningknowhow.com/special/xeriscape/xeriscape-principles-water-wise-gardening-tips.htm

Make Your Own Paper Fans
Here are some links to various ways to make paper fans:
https://www.youtube.com/watch?v=-OAhXeJu41g

https://www.youtube.com/watch?v=c8bv4W70Uc0

More about Washing Your Clothes by Hand:
https://www.sierraclub.org/sierra/step-step-guide-washing-your-clothes-hand

About Washboards: https://www.youtube.com/watch?v=SLDyMFlV2zU

Hand-cranked Washing Machines:
https://www.mentalfloss.com/article/502296/5-non-electric-washers-save-you-laundromat

Mangle Wringer:
https://www.lehmans.com/product/lehmans-best-hand-wringer?gclid=CjwKCAjw5Ij2BRBdEiwA-0Frc9YBkqnaIqNtCG91ehq0eI78FA2NBjugldU3X-sr-rc9fgI16xQMLHyRoCV14QAvD_BwE

CALCULATE YOUR CARBON FOOTPRINT HERE:

https://apps.apple.com/us/app/mathtappers-carbon-choices/id386999548

Make a Simple Solar Cooker:
https://www.youtube.com/watch?v=v5CdN-H3sQT0

Climate Careers:
https://climate.careers

Climate Activists Organizations: Join Up and Act Up!
https://www.greenpeace.org/usa/jane-fonda-fire-drill-fridays-for-the-climate/

https://www.sierraclub.org

https://350.org

https://www.ourchildrenstrust.org

https://climatemuseum.org

www.ingramcontent.com/pod-product-compliance
Lightning Source LLC
Chambersburg PA
CBHW050303010526
44108CB00040B/2251